FOLK SHADOW PLAY

FOLK
SHADOW PLAY

Compiled by Wei Liqun

FOREIGN LANGUAGES PRESS

First Edition 2008

ISBN 978-7-119-04670-9

Published by

Foreign Languages Press

24 Baiwanzhuang Road, Beijing 100037, China

http: //www. flp. com. cn

Distributed by

China International Book Trading Corporation

35 Chegongzhuang Xilu, Beijing 100044, China

P.O. Box 399, Beijing, China

Printed in the People's Republic of China

Contents

INTRODUCTION

Origin of the Shadow Play

The shadow play is a traditional folk dramatic art that is widespread in China. Its origin is said to date back to the Han Dynasty (206 BC - 220 AD), but it was not until the Song Dynasty (960-1279) that the art form had its earliest appearance in the records of historians.

Legend has it that Emperor Wu of the Han Dynasty (r. 140-88 BC) missed his deceased concubine, Lady Li, very much. A man claimed he could summon her ghost. At night, he moved a puppet in front of some lit candles to cast its shadows on a cloth curtain. From a distance, the emperor did indeed seem to see the shadow of Lady Li. This is said to be the earliest appearance of the shadow play.

Rich young man: Republic of China, Lulong County, Hebei

Daoist, whose soft cap designs show his magic power: Republic of China (1912-1949), Huaxian County, Shaanxi

General: Republic of China, Huaxian County, Shaanxi

Family guardian:
Republic of China, Huaxian
County, Shaanxi

Martial role: Republic of China,
Fengrun County, Hebei

Elderly: Republic of China,
Qinglong County, Hebei

The Chinese shadow play has its origins in the magic, shadow games and puppet shows during the Han and Tang (618-907) dynasties, as well as the storytelling of the Song Dynasty. In his *Sequel to the Notes for Understanding the Way*, Zhang Lei (1052-1112), a native of Huaiyin of the Northern Song Dynasty (960-1127), recorded: "There is a man from a rich family in the Capital... who loves watching shadow plays. Every time Guan Yu [a famous general of the Three Kingdoms period] is killed in the play, he weeps for him, and asks the puppeteer to hold the scene for a while." This is the earliest record concerning a shadow play.

Some historical books also mention the types of Song shadow plays and the designs of their puppets, as well as the structure of the industry. They tell that the earliest peak of the shadow play was from the 10th to the 13th century.

Genres of Chinese Shadow Play and Their Spread

After the shadow play took shape in the Central Plains area along the valley of the Yellow River, Bianjing (today's Kaifeng, Henan), capital of the Northern Song Dynasty, became the earliest center of the shadow play from where all genres of shadow play spread all over China.

In the later years of the dynasty, Jin troops conquered this city. They captured a number of shadow-play artisans, and later took them north. Some artisans fled westward out through the Tongguan Pass, to escape wars. Most others followed the Song court, moving to the south of China. As shadow-play artisans put down roots and developed the art in various areas, three shadow-play genres gradually formed in the northern, western, and central and southern regions.

The northern shadow play largely spread through east Hebei, northeast China, east Inner Mongolia, east Beijing and suburban Tianjin. The western shadow play became popular in areas like Shaanxi, Gansu, Qinghai, Sichuan, south Shanxi, east Henan, west Hubei, central Hebei and west Beijing. Whereas from Zhejiang, the central and southern shadow play also developed into south Hebei, Henan, Shandong, Hubei, Hunan, Fujian and Taiwan.

Many countries have shadow plays; yet its birthplace remains in China. It is widely recognized that Chinese shadow play was the earliest and most representative, among the many genres around the world. The shadow plays of India, Thailand, Burma, Indonesia and Japan were all developed later than that of China. The Czech Republic, Slovakia, and other European countries all acknowledge their shadow plays come from the East. In the 13th century, the Chinese shadow play spread to Persia and Turkey with China's expeditionary troops. In 1767, a French missionary took all types of Chinese shadow plays and the techniques of making puppets to France, giving public performances in Paris and Marseilles. In recent years, Chinese shadow-play troupes of different genres have visited Germany, France, the US, Holland and Japan.

Dragon King: Republic of China,
Fengrun County, Hebei

Tortoise spirit: Republic of
China, Fengrun County, Hebei

Carp spirit: Republic of China,
Fengrun County, Hebei

Shrimp spirit: Republic of China,
Fengrun County, Hebei

Throughout its long period of development, the Chinese shadow play has formed a complete system with obvious national features and high aesthetic value. When the shadow play spread to a region, it would absorb the elements of local dialect, opera and folk customs, and thereby develop a local style. The differences in the shadow plays of various regions are mainly manifested in the melodies. Since the puppet designs were not limited by dialect or local opera, they evolved very little in the process of wide spreading. In the early stages of the shadow play, puppets of different regions looked relatively uniform. It was not until the Qing Dynasty (1644-1911) that puppet designs took on regional features. Studies on the evolution process of the designs will help us understand the continuation of the plastic arts, as well as the interaction of shadow play art with local paintings, operas and customs.

Mussel spirit:
Republic of China, Fengrun
County, Hebei

Frog spirit:
Republic of China, Fengrun
County, Hebei

Crab spirit:
Republic of China, Fengrun
County, Hebei

Shadow Play and Folk Customs

There are many customs in the shadow-play performances of various regions. In Hunan, Shanxi, Shaanxi, Gansu, Qinghai, Fujian, Jiangsu and Zhejiang, a type of shadow play for divine veneration is very popular. Called "votive shadow play," it involves a ceremony of sacrifice and vows. Shadow plays are also performed on birthday parties, weddings or funerals. Such performances, intended for the amusement of both deities and people, are widespread all over China.

Just as peasants worship Shennong (legendary god of farming) and plasterers and carpenters worship Lu Ban (legendary master of woodcraft), shadow-play troupes have their own ancestors who they venerate. But as customs vary in different regions, the ancestor worship also differs. Troupes in Shaanxi and central Shanxi worship Li Longji, Emperor Xuanzong (r.712-756) of the Tang Dynasty (618-907); troupes in south Shanxi and Gansu worship Li Cunxu, Emperor Zhuangzong (r.923-26) of the Later Tang Dynasty (923-936); while those in Hebei and northeast China honor Bodhisattva Guanyin.

The troupes also have many rules and taboos. For example, with troupes of Hebei's Luanzhou (Luanxian County today), the drama scripts on their desks could not be touched by hand, as they believe this would tarnish these divine scriptures. Instead, they use bamboo flakes to leaf them. The troupes of Huaxian County, Shaanxi, never allow the jumbling of puppet heads and bodies of male and female characters, or putting puppets face to face because they believe this would cause quarrels and splits in the troupes. They also prohibit any sitting on the scripts, believing this would ruin their performances. Among the troupes in south Shanxi there are three taboos that could bring misfortune to the troupes: women are not allowed onstage; none others are allowed to touch the scripts except the performers; and no one is allowed to sit on the trunks containing stage props.

In east Hebei, Shanxi and Shaanxi, where shadow plays are popular, there's a custom – the shadow-play troupes are exempt from paying any ferry fees, but would perform shadow plays on the ferry in exchange. This is based on a tale.

Longevity design in a votive shadow play: Luanzhou, Hebei

A design wishing promotion and salary increase: Luanzhou, Hebei

Happiness design in a votive shadow play: Luanzhou, Hebei

A long, long time ago, a shadow-play troupe was crossing a river by ferry. When the boat was sailing mid-river, it suddenly sprung a leak. In the midst of the calamity, an artisan quickly used a castanet to block the hole. When the boat got to the bank, the troupe placed a plank by the ferry for its gangway. After that, all shadow-play artisans and ferrymen became good friends. Even to this day, the stage at a shadow play always lacks one plank, and a troupe only has three castanets. When ferrymen make new boats, they always lay a castanet-like wooden plug at the bottom of the boat. And still, shadow-play artisans never have to pay the fare on ferries.

There are two special puppets in the shadow-play performances of Luanzhou. The two "brothers" both have a big fan-like open hand and a small claw-like palm. They do not have specific roles in any play, but may appear onstage at any time. Legend says these two poor boys were abandoned in a temple and brought up by a monk. Later, when the monk became seriously ill, they went out to beg alms for him. They passed through villages and towns, gesturing and singing of the monk's merits and kindness, using a paper figure to represent him. Some senior artists recall this as the origin of the shadow play in Luanzhou.

Ceremonial worship in a votive shadow play: Qinglong County, Hebei

Memorial tablet worshipped
in a votive shadow play:
Qinglong County, Hebei

To venerate them, two puppets were made. During the intermission, they will appear on stage and act like clowns, making the audience laugh with their jokes. Sometimes they play as extras.

When the performance is over, all puppet heads are removed from their bodies and packed in rows by their categories. But these two puppet heads are never removed from their bodies, which implies they will never die. They are always placed on the top layer in the trunk of props. Instead of using donkey hide, these two are made of dog hide, since tradition claims that dog hide can repel evil spirits.

Puppet Designs

The designs are diverse. Among the props are always 100 to 200 puppet bodies, and several hundred puppet heads, as well as countless colored scenic backdrops.

The designs have different features according to region, but they all have a common tradition that endows heroes with attractive appearances, and villains ugly look. Influenced by local temple sculptures, murals and stage costumes, various stylized facial makeup and decorative designs were formed.

Old containers of puppet heads:
Republic of China, Yushu, Jilin

Ju Shang, a puppet carver from Lichang County, Hebei

Memorial tablet for deities
in the props trunk of a
shadow-play troupe in rural Hubei

Lang Zili, the fourth generation
leader of the Lang's Troupe in
Haining, Zhejiang

For example, the straight nose bridge, round eyebrows and narrow eyes of Guanyin in east Hebei are adopted in the facial makeup of positive *xiaodan* (young female), *xiaosheng* (young male) and *laosheng* (aged male) characters in shadow plays.

In east Shaanxi, the puppets are always exquisite. Attaching great importance to decorative and carving skills, puppets of *sheng* (male) and *dan* (female) characters in this area have protruding foreheads, delicate noses and small mouths. In contrast, the puppet designs in west Shaanxi are rough and forceful, with simple decorations. *Hualian* (painted-face) characters always have round noses and hollowed eyes, while *sheng* and *dan* characters' noses are straight and high.

Different from other puppets, Hubei's large puppets are incisive, with eyebrows and eyes painted, and with the hollows in some puppets' faces even decorated with color silk. Hubei also has delicate small puppets that are deeply influenced by the Shaanxi style.

The puppets in east and north Sichuan are delicate, similar to those in east Shaanxi; while in west Sichuan the puppets are always large and bulky, focusing on the portrayal of the personalities of characters.

In general, the puppet head offers a side view, with only five-tenths of it shown, while seven-tenths of its body is shown. This feature is called "five-tenths faces and seven-tenths costumes." To represent all features of the character in the design, this unique method is created to wonderfully combine different visual angles.

If only a puppet fits the plot's needs, it doesn't matter much whether it has polish. However, as rich families began supporting private shadow-play troupes, they hired professional carvers to make puppets, thereby producing a large number of highly skilled carvers and elegant art works.

Zhang Huazhou and his father Zhang Qi, puppet carvers of Huaxian County, Shaanxi

Wang Qiansong, a puppet carver of Xieqiao Town, Haining, Zhejiang

Carving and Color Drawing

Shaping and airing hide: by Lu Fuzeng of Fengrun County, Hebei

The material of puppets of the northern shadow play is mainly donkey hide, while that of the western and the central and southern shadow plays is often cowhide, and sheepskin, horse-hide, camel-hide or even thick paper are also used in some places.

Carving technique always requires great attention, as only with refined carving techniques can good designs be made. The steps, including hide processing, carving, coloring, oiling and assembly, are closely related. Among them, hide processing and carving are the key steps. Puppets treated with superb hide-processing techniques are still as smooth as new after a hundred years.

There are two methods for carving puppet heads: cameo and intaglio. Cameo carving is often used for the heads of *sheng* and *dan* characters. Smooth and forceful lines outline the faces. The background is cut away, leaving the features projected in relief, which look particularly sharp when their shadows are cast on the white curtain. Intaglio carving is used for the heads of bold and generous *jing* characters. Their features and headgear are cut into the heads and painted with different colors.

The knives used for carving puppets are highly specialized. There are always a dozen or even several dozen knives. In terms of carving skills, there are "running knife" skills that use knives like pens to carve lines into the hide, and "driving hide" skills that hold the hide in the hand to touch the knife edge to form designs according to outlines.

Shaving hide: by Lu Fuzeng   Shaved hide: by Lu Fuzeng

As a representative of Shaanxi's puppet carving, Li Zhanwen's works are so delicate that even the puppets' hair and beard are very clear. The most popular carver in east Hebei was Yang Desheng (1873-1942), whose works had concise designs and fresh compositions. His carving skill was exquisite: the puppets representing *sheng* and *dan* characters were handsome and pretty; the *jing* puppets had vivid features, always with nestling silkworm-like brows, Grecian noses and beards flowing in five locks. His movements were fluent and agile, and his technique of using knives, both large and small knife-edges, were deeply admired by other puppet carvers.

A puppet can always be divided into parts, such as the head, upper body, lower body, arms, legs, hands and feet. The number of joints varies. For instance, the puppets of fighting characters have more joints for easier movements. Many puppets of scholar characters in the Zhejiang area have only one arm; while the puppets of *dan* characters in Taiwan cannot separate their two feet.

Colors are used to enrich the puppet designs. The five traditional colors – red, yellow, blue, white and black – are well balanced in the designs. Yet in the northern shadow play, green is used instead of blue. This is because, under the light of oil lamps – the only illumination at night in ancient times – blue appears black. Moreover, the contrast between green and red is stronger than between blue and red, which makes the designs more vivid. The hollowed part looks white behind the curtain, and the original color of the hide is yellow, so in fact the only colors used are red, green and black. They are painted alternately along the carving lines.

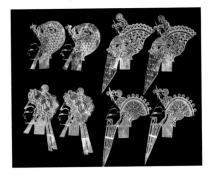

Carving puppets: by Lu Fuzeng

Semi-finished puppets, cut in pairs

Painting colors

Puppet designs by Yang Desheng

Preservation of the Shadow play

The shadow play is a distillation of China's opera. It represents the profound tradition of Chinese civilization, and also exercises a holistic influence on the development of other Chinese art forms.

Few other art forms can compare the shadow play as a folk art that has existed and prospered for a thousand years all over China. Different from the shadow plays of other countries, the Chinese genre not only has a long history, a variety of forms, a wide popularity and a rich tradition, but also a special capacity to integrate art design, literary scripts, music, tunes and performance techniques.

Traditional square table for eight people: Qing Dynasty, Leting County, Hebei

Carrying a bridal sedan-chair: Qing Dynasty, Luanzhou, Hebei

Elephant-drawn carriage for emperor's inspection tour:
Qing Dynasty, Qian'an, Hebei

Long table for placing decorations and books:
Qing Dynasty, Fengrun County, Hebei

As society develops, people's lifestyles change and new art forms become more popular, all these have led to the decline of traditional shadow plays. The older generation of shadow-play artisans is fading, but the middle-aged and especially young artisans have not increased accordingly. The shrinking of the audience, especially younger audience, also endangers this traditional art form.

The puppets pictured in this book are mostly collections of the author. Acknowledgement is also given to Mr. Wang Dingzhi and Mr. Li Hongjun of the Shaanxi Art Museum, folk-art researcher Mr. Zou Zhengzhong of Taiwan, and folk artist Mr. Tai Liping, for their generous support and help.

SHADOW PLAY
PERFORMANCE

Performers

Besides the differences in puppet designs, the performance of shadow plays also varies according to region. For instance, the shadow play in east Hebei and northeast China often call for seven or eight players: two are operators, while the others sing tunes and play percussion and string instruments. The shadow play in Shaanxi and Gansu needs four to six players: one is the main singer, who speaks and sings for all characters and plays *yueqin* (plucked instrument with a full-moon-shaped sound-box) and beats *tanggu* (drum) at the same time; another operates all the puppets on and off the stage; while the rest are accompanists. Shandong's shadow play needs the fewest players, with one operating all characters and singing tunes for them, and the other playing the slit-drum, drum and cymbals.

The props trunks of a shadow-play troupe in Wangcheng County, Hunan – always carried to the stage on a shoulder pole

Senior shadow-play artist Zhang Zhaobin from Baokang County, Hebei, could not find an apprentice to pass down his skills to.

Senior shadow-play artist Su Wenxiu, the most revered of players in south Hebei

Singing

All shadow plays around China do songs in local dialect and colloquial speech. While the puppets may look the same in a region, the tunes and dialects may vary a great deal. In many areas, shadow plays still use the traditional narrative style, enjoying a reputation of "narrating the vicissitudes of a thousand years on the stage" and "story-telling behind a curtain."

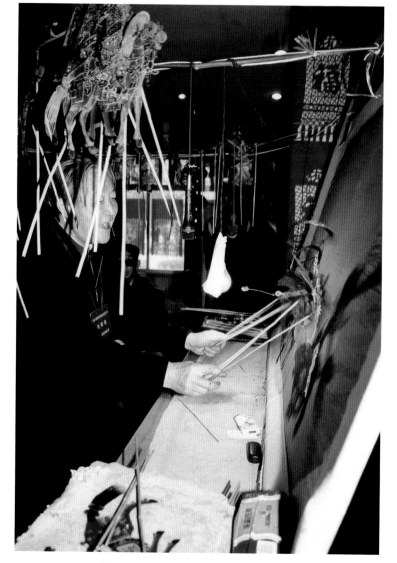

Shadow-play artist Wang Yunfei from Qishan County, Shaanxi,
performing in Nanjing

Lang Zili, the fourth generation leader of the
Lang's Troupe in Haining, Zhejiang

Master artist Ding Zhenyao from Tangshan,
Hebei, still sings as beautifully as ever

Senior shadow-play artist Lü Zuoliang,
from Tongxiang, Zhejiang, playing for tourists
in the river town Wuzhen

Senior shadow-play artist Lin Zhihai from Luoshan County,
Henan, preparing for his performance

Shadow-play performance

Stage

The shadow play's stage is always temporary, built with wooden poles and boards on higher ground. It is quite simple to build such a stage: erect several wooden poles (or use tree trunks) on a flat terrain first, then put boards on these poles to make a platform, set a white-cloth curtain in front of the platform, and finally use cloth curtains to enclose the backstage area. The shadow-play troupes in Fufeng, Shaanxi have even handier stages: either on a large cart, or on a flat piece of earth enclosed by matting.

Behind the curtain of a troupe
from Yutian County, Tangshan

Senior artisans from Cheng'an
County, Handan, arranging the
seldom-used puppets

Artisans from Cheng'an County,
building a stage for a show for
international guests

Shadow Play in South Hebei

Handan is the representative of the shadow play in south Hebei, which obviously inherited the characteristics of ancient shadow play. Made of cowhide, the puppets appear in an unsophisticated style; the carvings are not refined. In many places, color painting is used instead of carving. This combination of carving and painting is one of the features of this genre.

Most shadow-play artists in south Hebei are over age 60,
indicating the genre's decline.

Senior artisan Shen Guorui from
Cheng'an County, operating
puppets in *Journey to the West*

Ancient shadow-play stage in Yuanjia Village,
Weixian County, Hebei

Ancient Stages

Ancient shadow-play stages have been preserved both in Weixian County, Hebei and Xiaoyi County, Shanxi. The Yuanjia Village in Weixian has a specialized stage for shadow play back in those times. Facing north, the stage is 3.3 meters wide and 2 meters high. On the inner wall, there are notes recording the time of the shows, lists of plays and players from local troupes that had played here from the 17th to the mid-20th century.

In the court of the Xiaoyi Shadow Play and Puppet Show Museum, there are four stages for shadow plays and puppet shows, which were moved there for exhibition from nearby villages.

In the "Manchu Shadow Play Hall," in the Chengde Summer Resort, as well as at the shadow-play house in Wuzhen, Zhejiang, there are shadow-play troupes performing during the tourist season. In the five teahouses in Yunmeng County of Hubei, shadow plays are performed from 11:30 to 14:30 every day all year round.

Shadow Play Performance

The shadow play is a type of puppet show. Through the coordination of singers and operators, the dubbed speaking and singing of the actors can impress and move the audience. The actors try to imbue their understanding of the characters' feelings and emotions into the performance. In this way do the puppets come alive.

What's on at Mengze Shadow Play Hall today?

Mengze Shadow Play Hall in Yunmeng County, Hubei, has a full house every day.

Feng Chengxian, a shadow-play percussion musician from Qinhuangdao

King of the Rod

Qi Yongheng (1933 -) is a gifted shadow-play operator. His greatest claim to fame is his excellent skills in manipulating puppets. He hails from a family of shadow players, and with his father, began manipulating the puppets at eight. He has worked for the Tangshan Shadow Play Troupe since the 1950s. He is called "Qi, the living shadow play puppet" and "King of the Rod" among the locals. International audiences have appraised his manipulation as "a magic and lightning art."

Legend of the White Snake –
a shadow play in Tangshan

The Skillfully Made-up Witch –
a shadow play in Tangshan

Romance on Two Mountains –
a shadow play in Tangshan

A curious peep under the curtain

Tung-Hua, a shadow puppet show troupe
of Taiwan

Master Qi Yongheng, reigning
"King of the Rod"

Qi Yongheng performs with Qi Yongqing
and Da Jianguang

Troupe leaders Qin Ligang (top) and Teng Deqing, of the
"Mengze Shadow Play Hall," well coordinated

PUPPET DESIGNS IN
THE WESTERN SHADOW PLAY

Sets

Shadow Play Sets in Shaanxi

The peak of Shaanxi's shadow play was between the late 19th and early 20th centuries. As officials and the wealthy loved shadow plays, many professional puppet workshops were established. The refined puppets, made in those workshops with great care, are unparalleled in their artistry.

The scenery in Shaanxi's shadow plays include pavilions, towers, storied buildings, grottoes and caves, paradise and hell. With great imagination, the artisans have produced various wonderful images of figures and animals, which have not only enriched the content of shows and performance effects, but also displayed the romantic traditions of China's folk arts.

Blackwater River – a shadow-play scene from Dali County: Shaanxi Art Museum

Monkey King's Inspection – a shadow-play scene from Dali County: Shaanxi Art Museum

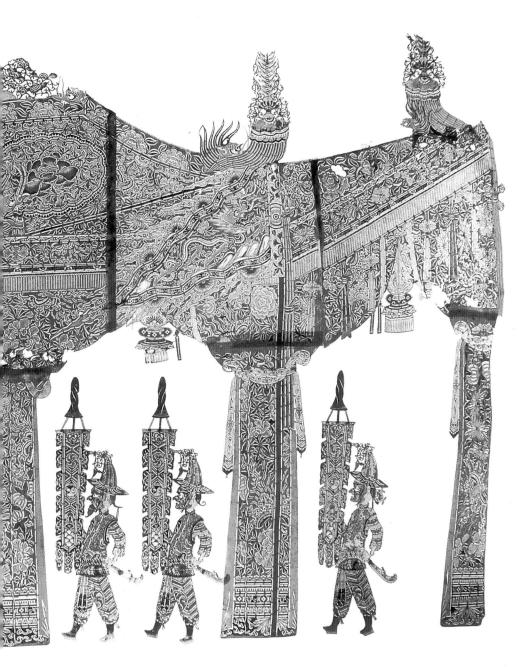

Fan Lihua Takes Command – the story of a woman general
of the Tang Dynasty: Dali County, Shaanxi Art Museum

Xie Yaohuan – the story of a gifted and upright imperial maid
of the Tang Dynasty: Dali County, Shaanxi Art Museum

The Buddha Explains the Scriptures: Dali County,
Shaanxi Art Museum

Journey to the West – four monks going west to find the Buddhist scriptures and truths: Dali County, Shaanxi Art Museum

The West Chamber – the romantic tale of a couple who were ultimately married, after overcoming many obstacles: Dali County, Shaanxi Art Museum

Whole Puppets

Acrobatic Designs

The Shaanxi shadow play carvers often have the warhorses connected with their riders, with active joints, being known as "horse armor." There are also "kylin armor," "elephant armor," "tiger armor," "camel armor" and "donkey armor." This carving method makes it easier to perform fight scenes of horse-riding warriors, and one operator alone even can manipulate the fighting.

Horse-riding marshal: Qing
Dynasty, collected by Tai Liping
of Fengxiang County, Shaanxi

Honor guard at court: carved by Zhang Huazhou
of Huaxian County, Shaanxi

Facial Makeup in Shaanxi Shadow Play

An outstanding feature of the facial makeup in Shaanxi's shadow play is the protruding foreheads of all characters, whether they are *sheng* (male), *dan* (female), *jing* (painted face) or *chou* (clown), which makes the puppets look impressive and grand. The puppets in eastern Shaanxi are small, standing only 29 to 33 cm high. *Xiaosheng* (young male) and *xiaodan* (young female) characters always have straight noses and small mouths. The audience can easily tell the characters through their eyebrows: level eyebrows indicate scholarly characters, who are quiet and comely; while erect eyebrows indicate fighting and generals, who are doughty and bold.

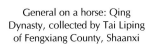

General on a horse: Qing Dynasty, collected by Tai Liping of Fengxiang County, Shaanxi

Honor guard of court maidens:
carved by Zhang Huazhou of Huaxian County, Shaanxi

Puppet Heads of *Dan* Characters

Sheng, Dan, Jing, Chou Characters in Chinese Operas

Chinese operas have four basic types of characters: *sheng*, *dan*, *jing* and *chou*. *Sheng* are male characters, except for male *jing* and *chou*; *dan* refer to all female characters; *jing*, also called "painted faces," are bold or generous characters with facial makeup and resonant voices; *chou*, called "little painted faces," behave like clowns. The audience can easily judge the gender, age, social status, features and personalities of each character according to their respective character type.

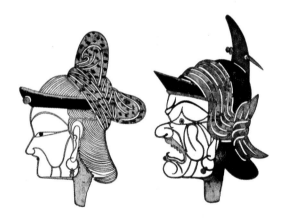

Aged women: Republic of China,
Huaxian County, Shaanxi

Aged women: Qing Dynasty, Beijing

Dan

Dan roles cover all female characters in Chinese opera, and can be divided into seven categories – *zhengdan, huadan, tiedan, guimendan, wudan, laodan* and *caidan*.

Lady White Snake: Republic of China, Huaxian County, Shaanxi

Zhengdan: middle-aged or young modest and forthright female characters

Huadan: middle-aged or young lively or dissolute female characters, contrasted with *zhengdan*

Tiedan: minor female roles, not indicating a distinctive personality

Guimendan: young girls

Wudan: female characters skilled at martial arts

Laodan: senior women

Caidan: female clowns

Emperor's concubine, with showy hair ornaments: Republic of China, Huaxian County, Shaanxi

Puppet Heads of *Sheng* Characters

Except for *jing* and *chou* characters, all males in Chinese operas are *sheng* characters, in categories such as *laosheng*, *xiaosheng*, *jinsheng*, *guansheng*, *qiongsheng*, *zhiweisheng*, *wuxiaosheng* and *wusheng*.

Zhuangyuan (Number One Scholar in the imperial examination): Qing Dynasty, Huaxian County, Shaanxi

Laosheng: middle-aged or older upright characters, also called *xusheng* as they always wear beards (*xu*)

Xiaosheng: young men

Jinsheng: handsome young scholars wearing *jin* (scholar's cap) or carrying fans (*shanzi*, hence the name *shanzisheng*)

Guansheng are divided into *daguansheng* and *xiaoguansheng*. The former are often a bearded emperor or unruly scholars, and the latter are young nobilities.

Qiongsheng: impoverished scholars

Warrior: Republic of China, Huaxian County, Shaanxi

Zhiweisheng, or *lingzisheng*: the name derives from the two *zhiwei* (or *lingzi*, pheasant feathers) on the helmet

Wuxiaosheng: young generals

Wusheng: male characters skilled at martial arts

Headgear

The headgear used in traditional Chinese operas may be divided into four categories – *guan, kui, jin* and *mao* – with variously affixed decorations, the types totaling over 300. Like stage costumes, the headgear differs according to the plays and operas. *Guan* is the formal cap of an emperor or noble characters. *Kui* is the helmet of warriors and generals. *Jin* is a type of informal soft cap. *Mao* is the most complicated one, including *suluomao* (black silk cap) by common folk such as family servants, and *hualuomao* (color silk cap) with embroidered balls, worn by swordsmen.

Poor young man:
Republic of China, Huaxian
County, Shaanxi

Tang Priest in Ming-dynasty
novel *Journey to the West*:
Republic of China, Huaxian
County, Shaanxi

Young scholar:
Qing Dynasty, Huaxian
County, Shaanxi

Senior official:
Huaxian County, Shaanxi

Puppet Heads of *Jing* Characters

Jing

Jing characters are also called *hualian* (painted faces). This type of roles always has a resonant voice, representing their bold and generous personalities. *Jing* are almost always positive characters, though occasionally also villains.

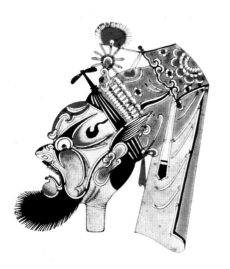

General with a painted face: Republic of China, Huaxian County, Shaanxi

General with a painted face: Qing Dynasty, Huaxian County

Puppet Heads of *Jing* Characters in Shaanxi Shadow Play

The facial makeup of *jing* characters in Shaanxi's shadow play is quite elaborate. For example, the image of Zhang Fei, a bold general of the Shu Kingdom during the Three Kingdoms period (220-280), has a leopard-like head and big round eyes; the image of Guan Yu, another general of the Shu Kingdom, portrays his uprightness through his silkworm-like brows and sloping eyes; while the images of resourceful military officers like Zhou Yu of the Wu Kingdom are shaped handsomely.

Villains and bad characters are commonly molded in a derogatory way. Take the facial makeup of Cao Cao, a statesman of the Wei Kingdom, as an example: there is always a rising point in the inner corner of his eye, and a red snake-like line on the lower orb, showing his ruthlessness. Another example is the chief eunuch who also has a red snake-like line on the lower orb and a snake-like black eyebrow.

Through their long periods of practice, puppet carvers have summarized some "general rules" for memorizing. For male characters, level eyes and brows represent their loyalty, and round open eyes indicate their boldness and fierceness; rising mouth corners indicate smiling, whereas knitted brows signal an anxious expression. Female characters require curly brows, line-like eyes, cherry-like small mouths; round foreheads, tapering chins and earrings. The features of the eyes often reveal the character's temperament: with level eyes and brows, the character is loyal; with round eyes, fierce; with line-like eyes, tame; while eyes like a leopard's show a bad temper.

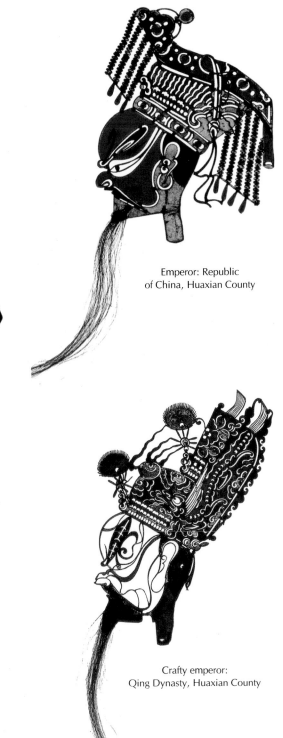

Emperor: Republic
of China, Huaxian County

Military man with
long whiskers:
Republic of China,
Huaxian County

Crafty emperor:
Qing Dynasty, Huaxian County

Puppet Designs in the Western Shadow Play

Family guard:
Republic of China, Huaxian County

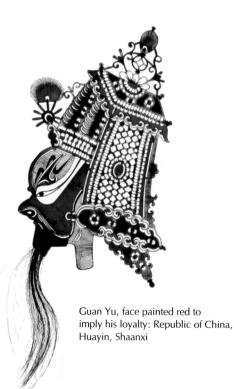

Guan Yu, face painted red to
imply his loyalty: Republic of China,
Huayin, Shaanxi

Marshal: Qing Dynasty,
Huaxian County, Shaanxi

Official wearing a gauze cap:
Qing Dynasty, Huaxian County

Tribe chief: Republic of
China, Huaxian County

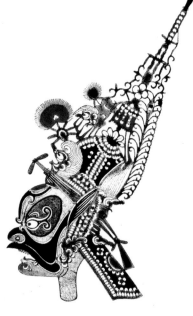

General: Republic of China,
Huaxian County

Evil general with a thick
beard: Republic of
China, Huaxian County

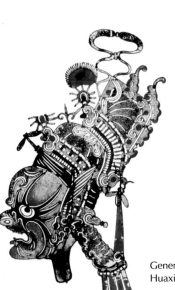

General: Republic of China,
Huaxian County

Puppet Heads of *Chou* Characters

Chou

Chou characters in Chinese operas are actually clowns, also called *xiaohualian* (little painted faces), whose nose bridge and eyeholes are painted with white powder.

They can be wise and humorous positive roles or villains; there are two categories: *wenchou* (civilian clown) and *wuchou* (warrior clown), with the former including *paodaichou*, *fangjinchou* and *laochou*.

Paodaichou: so named because of the ceremonial robe (*pao*) and jade belt (*dai*) worn by the characters, often humorous emperors, princes, officials and generals

Eunuch: Qing Dynasty,
Chengdu, Sichuan

Official: Qing Dynasty,
Chengdu, Sichuan

Official wearing a gauze cap:
Qing Dynasty, Huaxian County,
Shaanxi

Judge: Qing Dynasty,
Huaxian County, Shaanxi

Fangjinchou: so named because the characters often wear a square soft cap (*fangjin*), often humorous Confucians, advisors and copy clerks

Laochou: kind and humorous elderly

Wuchou: humorous and cunning characters adept in martial arts, with clear and fluent speaking

Deities and Spirits

Pig spirit:
Huaxian County, Shaanxi

Double-faced legendary evil minister:
Republic of China, Huaxian County

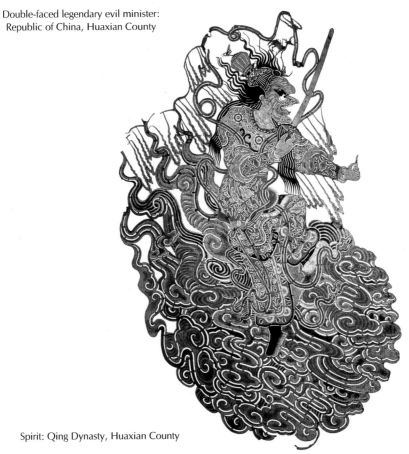

Spirit: Qing Dynasty, Huaxian County

Spirit: Qing Dynasty, Huaxian County

God of Wind:
Qing Dynasty, Huaxian County

God of Wealth:
Qing Dynasty, Huaxian County

Deity: Qing Dynasty, Huaxian County

Deity: Qing Dynasty, collected by Tai
Liping of Huaxian County, Shaanxi

Characters from the novel *Creation of the Gods*:
Ming Dynasty, Xiaoyi, Shanxi

Deity on a black tiger:
carved by Zhang Huazhou of Huaxian County, Shaanxi

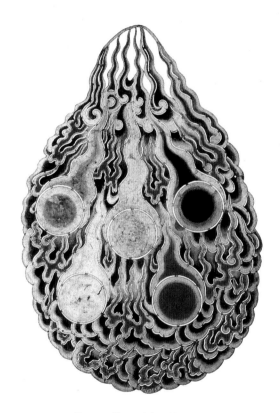

The sun: Shaanxi Arts Museum

PUPPET DESIGNS IN
THE NORTHERN SHADOW PLAY

Whole Puppets

The northern shadow play is a large system, with every troupe having over a hundred puppet bodies, wearing costumes classified into such categories as *kao*, *kai*, *mang*, *shan*, *pao*, *chang* and *yi*.

Kao is the armor of generals and soldiers, with flags on the back.

Kai is another kind of armor of military officers, who often wear a yellow *magua* (mandarin jacket worn over a gown) but no flags on the back.

Mang is the ceremonial robe of emperors, princes, generals and ministers: yellow for emperors, white for aged loyal ministers, black for black-faced or evil ministers, red and green for common ministers.

Woman with coiled buns of hair:
Qing Dynasty, Fengrun County

Aged woman in gorgeous clothes:
Qing Dynasty, Fengrun County

Woman general:
Qing Dynasty, Fengrun County, Hebei

Empress dowager:
early 20th century,
Fengrun County

Shan is an unlined upper garment, colored or black.

Chang is a cloak or mantle.

Yi includes an immortal's garments, a robe with the Eight Diagrams design, a monk's cassock, jail uniforms, and mourning clothes. There are also clothes fitted for acrobatic movements, as well as children's clothes.

Emperor puppets wear a sky-towering crown, and a robe with a yellow dragon design. Ministers wear *mang* and a gauze cap. Junior officials wear a black gauze cap and a uniform with rank insignia on the front and back. Field officers wear yellow *magua*. If a puppet wears a cloak and a hood, it must be on a journey. If it has a scarf wrapping its head and wears a white skirt, it must be ill.

An apparent difference between male and female puppets is their shoes: male roles wear boots while female always wear bowed shoes, and some aged *chou* women wear embroidered shoes for unbound feet.

Swordsman, wearing a color cap
with silk balls: Qing Dynasty,
Fengrun County, Hebei

Soldier: Qing Dynasty,
Funing County, Hebei

Martial man with a painted face:
Qing Dynasty, Leting County, Hebei

Frowning marshal:
early 20th century, Changli County, Hebei

Red-faced swordsman wearing
a simple silk cap: Qing Dynasty,
Changli County, Hebei

Aged marshal:
Republic of China,
Qian'an, Hebei

Puppet Designs in the Northern Shadow Play

Woman marshal:
Qing Dynasty, Funing County, Hebei

Shehuo Set Designs

In the northern shadow play, there are many set designs depicting *shehuo* performances, village festive activities such as dragon lantern dance, lion dance, pushing floats, "land boat" dance, *yangge* dance, dance on stilts, and riding performance. To the accompaniment of musical instruments like *suona* horn, these scenes appear when there are temple fairs depicted in a shadow play.

Horseback acrobatics:
Republic of China, carved by Ruan Guizhong

Pushing floats: Republic of China,
carved by Ruan Guizhong of Fengrun County, Hebei

"Land boat" dance: Republic of China,
carved by Ruan Guizhong

Ne Zha on the wheels of cloud and fire:
Qinhuangdao, Hebei

General in scale-mail armor:
Republic of China,
Luanxian County, Hebei

Woman marshal:
Republic of China,
Tangshan, Hebei

Legend of the White Snake

The classical play *Legend of the White Snake* also has shadow-play versions. The puppets of Xu Xian, Lady White Snake and Monk Fahai exhibited here were designed in the 1950s by northern shadow play troupes, bearing some characteristics of costumes from local operas of that time.

The *Legend of the White Snake* tells of a white and a green snake spirit on Mt. Emei who magically turn themselves into two girls called Bai Suzhen and Xiao Qing, and travel to West Lake. There Bai Suzhen falls in love with Xu Xian at first sight, and marries him with the help of Xiao Qing. Monk Fahai from the Jinshan Temple tries to sever the marriage. He confuses Xu Xian's mind and makes him leave home for the temple. To get her husband back, Bai Suzhen fights with Fahai. Though Xu Xian comes to himself later and is reconciled with Bai Suzhen, Fahai still uses his magic power to trap Bai Suzhen in the Leifeng Pagoda. Xiao Qing prays for help from a deity, and finally burns down the Pagoda and rescues Bai Suzhen.

Lady White Snake in a Daoist robe:
work of Hebei Changli Shadow Play Troupe

Fahai in cassock:
work of Hebei Changli Shadow Play Troupe

Xu Xian in a scholar's robe:
work of Hebei Changli Shadow Play Troupe

Young warrior: Republic of China,
Fengrun County, Hebei

Aged prime minister in white *mang* robe:
Republic of China, Yutian County, Hebei

Girl in a court dress:
Qing Dynasty, Yushu, Jilin

Middle-aged shrewish woman:
Qing Dynasty, Yushu, Jilin

Puppet Heads of *Dan* Characters

The emphasis is on the puppets' ornamentation, and this is closely related to the dramatic needs and aesthetic tastes of the northern audience. As the puppets are flat, they must be designed in an exaggerative and distorted, concise way to manifest the relations of the characters in the play. In general, puppets of *xiaosheng* (young male) and *xiaodan* (young female) characters have hollowed faces. A high nose bridge represents the side face line from forehead to nose tip. The brow connects with the eye, forming a circle. The mouth is only a short red line, and the chin is at a right angle. Headgear, coiled buns of hair, and earrings are the main differences between male and female characters.

Besides white-faced ones, there are also red-faced, black-faced and green-faced (evil) *dan* characters.

Evil woman:
carved by Xiao Fucheng
of Changli County, Hebei

Girl: carved by Zhao Guang'en
of Fengnan, Hebei

Daoist priestess:
Republic of China,
carved by Liu Jicheng of
Fengrun County, Hebei

Ornaments on Puppet Heads

The ornaments on puppet heads tell the social status of the characters. Take *dan* characters for example: if a puppet wears a phoenix-shaped crown, she must be a princess or an imperial concubine. Ordinary women have only hair buns or flowers as headgear; maidservants have their hair in a single bun or two coiled hair buns. The Daoist priestess often has a large leaf on her head, showing she is practicing Daoism in the depths of a mountain.

Aged woman:
Qing Dynasty, Yushu, Jilin

Young woman:
Republic of China,
Luanxian County,
Hebei

Aged woman:
Republic of China,
Fengrun County, Hebei

Woman wearing a phoenix-
shaped crown:
Republic of China, Liaoning

Woman wearing a phoenix headgear
to indicate her nobility:
Qing Dynasty,
carved by Yang Desheng of
Funing County, Hebei

Empress Wu Zetian:
Republic of China, Shenyang, Liaoning

Woman wearing
a phoenix-shaped crown:
carved by Lu Fuzeng of Fengrun
County, Hebei

Swordswoman:
carved by Zhao Guang'en
of Fengnan, Hebei

Daoist priestess: Republic of China,
carved by Ruan Guizhong of Fengrun
County, Hebei

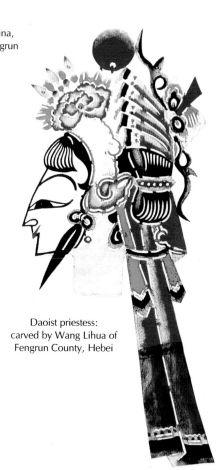

Daoist priestess:
carved by Wang Lihua of
Fengrun County, Hebei

Girl: carved by
Zhao Guang'en of
Fengnan, Hebei

Young woman with
two coiled hair buns:
carved by Liu Tianzeng
of Tangshan, Hebei

Girl: Republic of China,
carved by Ruan Guizhong of
Fengrun County, Hebei

Woman general: Qing Dynasty,
Fengrun County, Hebei

Court attendant: Qing Dynasty,
Leting County, Hebei

Woman: Yutian County, Hebei

Young woman: Republic of China,
carved by Ruan Guizhong of Fengrun
County, Hebei

Evil woman: Republic of China,
Yutian County, Hebei

Woman with a hairdo popular
among Manchu women:
carved by Xiao Fucheng of Changli
County, Hebei

Unattractive maid: Republic of China,
Changli County, Hebei

Woman marshal: Republic of China,
Qinglong County, Hebei

Woman wearing a phoenix-shaped
crown, whose face is flushed,
indicating she may have fainted:
1911, Yushu, Jilin

Alluring woman, wearing a
flower-shaped hairpin: Qing Dynasty,
Yushu, Jilin

Puppet Designs in the Northern Shadow Play

Puppet Heads of *Sheng* Characters

Middle-aged man:
Republic of China, carved by
Ruan Guizhong

Martial man, wearing a soft cap with
a fish-tail design: Republic of China,
carved by Ruan Guizhong

Cowherd: Republic of China,
carved by Ruan Guizhong of
Fengrun County, Hebei

Prime minister: Qing Dynasty,
carved by Yang Desheng of
Funing County, Hebei

General: carved by Lu Fuzeng of Fengrun
County, Hebei

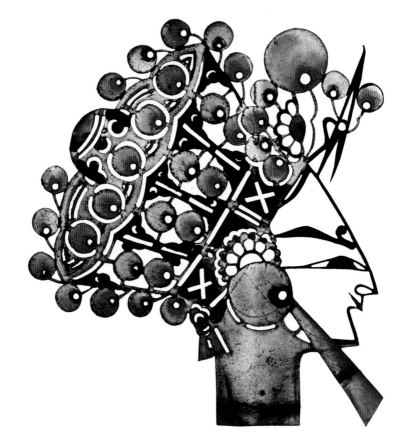

Frowning young man wearing a color silk cap:
Fengrun County, Hebei

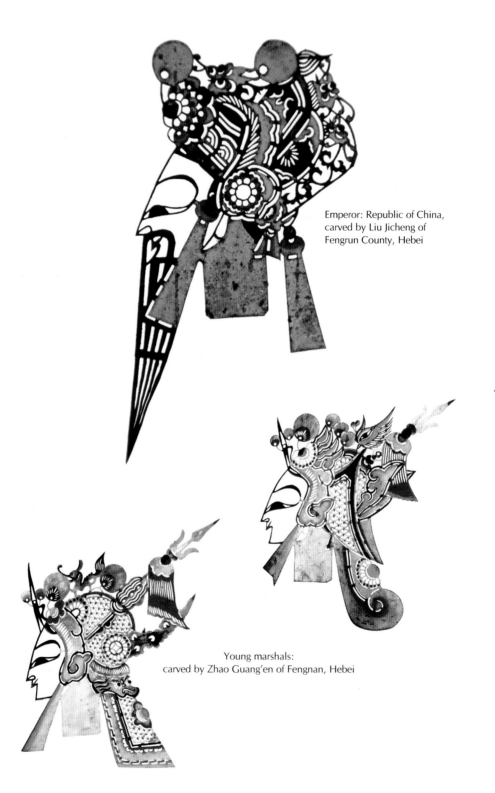

Emperor: Republic of China,
carved by Liu Jicheng of
Fengrun County, Hebei

Young marshals:
carved by Zhao Guang'en of Fengnan, Hebei

Senior marshal: Qing Dynasty,
Yushu, Jilin

Dandy young man:
Qing Dynasty, Yushu, Jilin

Dandy young man:
Qing Dynasty, Leting County, Hebei

Marshal: Qing Dynasty: Leting County, Hebei

Puppet Works of Ruan Guizhong

During the Republic of China (1912-1949), the works of Ruan Guizhong (1889-1970), a shadow-play puppet carver from Fengrun County, Hebei, were representative of the plays in west Tangshan. Ruan engaged in this art throughout his whole life. He placed much emphasis on auspicious decorations. Thanks to his masterly skills in using knives, his puppets are handsome and pretty and wouldn't be bent, deformed, or discolored despite the smoke and heat of lamps. People were very fond of his works, especially those carved between his 50s and 60s, during which time he left a large number of precious unpainted puppets.

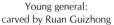
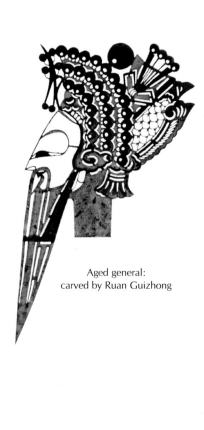

Aged general:
carved by Ruan Guizhong

Young general:
carved by Ruan Guizhong

Prince: carved
by Ruan Guizhong

Minority chieftain,
wearing some plumes:
carved by Ruan Guizhong

Puppet Works of Yang Desheng

Yang Desheng (1873-1942), of Hebei's Funing County, was another representative puppet carver of the northern shadow play. In those years, many troupes rushed to buy his puppets. His works were concise in design, fresh in composition, and exquisite in their carving. The puppets of *xiaosheng* and *xiaodan* characters are all good-looking, while the puppets of *jing* characters all have nestling silkworm-like brows, handsome noses, and beards with five locks. His carving strokes were agile, and he used both large and small knives. In his later years Yang led a destitute life.

Prince: carved by
Yang Desheng

Prince: carved by
Yang Desheng

General: carved by
Yang Desheng

General: carved by
Yang Desheng

Chivalrous swordsman:
carved by Yang Desheng

General wearing a lotus-leaf-shaped helmet: carved by Zhu Baolin of Zunhua, Hebei

Colors of Facial Designs

Great emphasis is placed on portraying the personalities of characters, and there is a tradition of "endowing loyal and upright characters with handsome looks, and ruthless or evil characters with ugly looks" since the Song Dynasty.

There is a set of stylized facial makeup and decorative designs used in the northern shadow play. The colors are similar to those of other Chinese operas. For example, red faces are related to loyalty and daring, and black faces represent virtue; while white faces mean duplicity, and bandits and spirits always have green faces.

Zhang Fei, a famous general
of the Three Kingdoms:
carved by Liu Tianzeng of Tangshan, Hebei

Guan Yu, a loyal general
of the Three Kingdoms:
carved by Liu Tianzeng of
Tangshan, Hebei

Puppet Heads of *Jing* Characters

Marshal, whose whiskers in three threads: carved by Xiao Fucheng of Changli County, Hebei

Chivalrous swordsman: Republic of China, Funing County, Hebei

General: Qing Dynasty, carved by Wang Zhongtian of Funing County, Hebei

General wearing
a lotus-leaf-shaped helmet:
Republic of China,
Qian'an, Hebei

Rebel general,
wearing whiskers in five locks and
a lotus-leaf-shaped helmet:
Qing Dynasty, Qian'an, Hebei

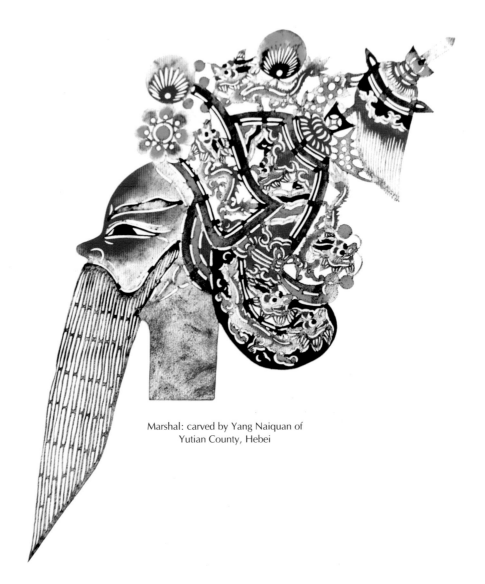

Marshal: carved by Yang Naiquan of
Yutian County, Hebei

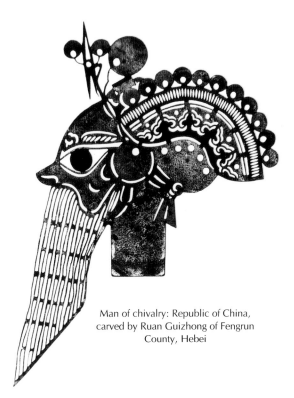

Man of chivalry: Republic of China,
carved by Ruan Guizhong of Fengrun
County, Hebei

Bao Zheng, an upright official
in ancient China: Qing Dynasty,
carved by Wang Zhongtian of Funing
County, Hebei

Guan Yu, whose face is
always painted red to signify his loyalty:
Republic of China,
carved by Ruan Guizhong of
Fengrun County, Hebei

Young general:
Republic of China, carved by Ruan
Guizhong of
Fengrun County, Hebei

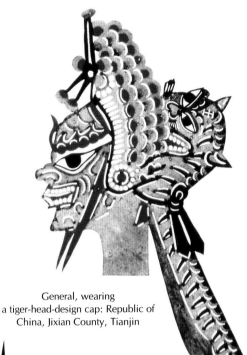

General, wearing
a tiger-head-design cap: Republic of
China, Jixian County, Tianjin

Zhang Fei, a bold general
of the Three Kingdoms: Republic of China,
carved by Ruan Guizhong of Fengrun
County, Hebei

Marshal with long white whiskers:
Qing Dynasty, Fengrun County, Hebei

General: Qing Dynasty,
carved by Yang Desheng of
Funing County, Hebei

Guan Yu with whiskers in
five locks: Republic of China,
Qinglong County, Hebei

Puppet Heads of *Chou* Characters

Marshals: Qing Dynasty, carved by Yang Desheng of
Funing County, Hebei

Marshals: Qing Dynasty, Yushu, Jilin

Wealthy man: Qing Dynasty, Yushu, Jilin

Martial man: Republic of
China, Yutian County, Hebei

Aged man wearing a felt cap:
Qing Dynasty, Yushu, Jilin

Puppet Heads of Evil Characters

To express the moral qualities of characters, puppet carvers lay emphasis on the puppets' eyes, brows, beard, and hair and cap styles. In the northern shadow play, evil characters, referred to as "large white face," always have a protruding nose, a large mouth, broom-like brows and some horizontal lines on the face, distinguishing them from the straight noses of *dan* and *sheng* characters. This technique of expression accords with the Chinese aesthetic sensibility, and the mass judgment of morality.

General with a curly beard and wearing
a fish tail-shaped cap: Republic of China,
Fengrun County, Hebei

Evil aged landlord with thick beard:
Republic of China, Liaoning

Evil martial man wearing a ducktail-
shaped cap with ornaments:
Republic of China, carved by Ruan
Guizhong of Fengrun County, Hebei

Evil prime minister with a thick beard:
Republic of China, Leting County, Hebei

Evil playboy with a curly beard:
Republic of China, carved by
Ruan Guizhong of Fengrun
County, Hebei

Evil man adept in martial arts:
Republic of China, carved by
Ruan Guizhong of Fengrun
County, Hebei

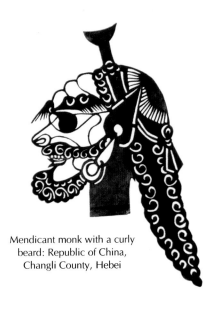

Mendicant monk with a curly
beard: Republic of China,
Changli County, Hebei

Martial man with a red curly beard: Republic
of China, Changli County, Hebei

Evil marshal with a thick beard:
Qing Dynasty, Changli County, Hebei

Deities and Spirits

In the northern shadow play, a puppet could be used in different plays to represent various characters of the same type. Only a few puppets are made for particular characters. For example, the puppet of a woman wearing a crown must be Tang Empress Wu Zetian; the puppet with two small hands sprouting from its eyes could only be Yang Ren in the *Creation of the Gods*; and the puppets of Tang Priest, Monkey, Pig and others in *Journey to the West* are also exclusive to these characters. These puppets could not be used to represent other characters, nor replaced by other puppets.

Deity of Fire: Qing Dynasty, Qian'an, Hebei

Thousand-handed Guanyin: Qing Dynasty,
Qian'an, Hebei

Monk: Qing Dynasty,
Shenyang

Yang Ren, whose eyes were cut out
after his loyal advice annoyed the
emperor, was saved by a deity, who
gave him a pair of hands with eyes on
the palms: Republic of China,
Qian'an, Hebei

Father Thunder:
Republic of China, Shenyang

Immortal Long-brow:
Qing Dynasty, Qian'an,
Hebei

Deity of Land:
Republic of China, Shenyang

Daoist priestess:
Republic of China, Shenyang

God of Longevity: early 20th century,
Fengrun County, Hebei

Deity warrior: carved by Xiao Fucheng
of Changli County, Hebei

Tang Priest in *Journey to the West*, same as
Monkey, Pig and Friar Sand:
carved by Lu Fuzeng of Fengrun County, Hebei

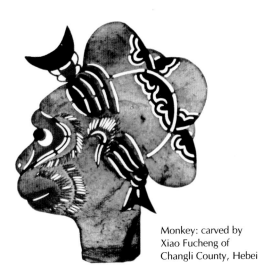

Monkey: carved by
Xiao Fucheng of
Changli County, Hebei

Pig: Qing Dynasty, Tangshan, Hebei

Friar Sand: Republic of China,
Zunhua, Hebei

Dragon King: carved by Liu Tianzeng of
Tangshan, Hebei

PUPPET DESIGNS IN
THE CENTRAL AND SOUTHERN
SHADOW PLAY

Whole Puppets

After the capital of the Northern Song Dynasty was conquered in 1127, all kinds of artists moved south to Lin'an (today's Hangzhou, Zhejiang), following the royal court. During the Southern Song Dynasty (1127-1279), various art forms thrived even more than they had in Bianjing (capital of the Northern Song, today's Kaifeng, Henan). The shadow play also reached its peak during this period.

At the beginning, Zhejiang's shadow-play puppets were made of color-painted sheepskin, which was gradually replaced by color-painted cowhide, both had strong decorative function and local flavor. This genre gives more weight to color painting than to carving, which is manifested by Haining's puppets of the Qing Dynasty. Generally, a puppet is 40 cm high. Except for the few used in acrobatic and fighting scenes that have two moveable arms and legs, most puppets have only one arm, and two unseparated legs.

Aged woman: Republic of China,
collected by Wang Qiansong of
Haining, Zhejiang

Puppets of the Mengze Shadow Play Hall: carved by Qin Ligang

Puppet Heads

Shadow plays in Lingbao, western Henan, and Tongbai and Luoshan in southern Henan, are representative of Henan's shadow play. The puppet designs in the Luoshan area are simple, with little carving but more emphasis on color painting. The puppets are 56.7 cm high, and their makeup is designed in a realistic way, and their caps are always separated from heads. The puppets popular in Hubei's Jingzhou and Mianyang areas, called "Door God figures," are large and austere in their carving. They represent an old tradition of realism.

Minority official: Qing Dynasty,
collected by Wang Qiansong

Young prime minister: Republic of
China, collected by Wang Qiansong

Military character: Republic of China,
Haining, Zhejiang

Official: Republic of China,
collected by Wang Qiansong

Military character: Qing Dynasty,
Haining, Zhejiang

Warrior: Qing Dynasty,
collected by Wang Qiansong of Haining, Zhejiang

OTHER SHADOW
PLAY DESIGNS

Auspicious Animals

Coming Out First

In Chinese legend, *ao* is a divine fish. In remote times, golden and silver carps tried to leap over the dragon gate to become flying dragons; however, some mistakenly ate the pearl in the sea, and could only become *ao*, with a dragon's head and a fish's body. It was said that when *ao* blinked, there were earthquakes; if they turned over, heaven would collapse and the earth sink.

Another tale says that once a young man went to the capital to take the imperial exam. While passing the Land of Women, this handsome man was accosted by a group of women. In a panic, he jumped into the sea, but was fortunately saved by an *ao*. Later when he scored first in the imperial exam, he went to the seaside to thank the *ao* for its kind aid. The beaming young man jumped onto the *ao*'s head and danced happily, hence the saying "taking only the ao's head," meaning "coming out first."

Lion: Qing Dynasty, Fengrun County, Hebei

Kylin: Qing Dynasty, Yutian County, Hebei

Dragon: Republic of China, collected by
Zheng Quanming of Linyi County, Shandong

Ox: Qing Dynasty, Qian'an, Hebei

Fire dragon: Qing Dynasty, Fengxiang County, Shaanxi

Ao: Qing Dynasty, Huaxian County, Shaanxi

Crane-riding boy: Republic of China,
Fengrun County, Hebei

Divine deer: Republic of China,
Fengrun County, Hebei

Furniture Designs

Auspicious Connotations

Auspicious connotations have always been the core of Chinese design. Using puns or wordplay, folk artisans imbue auspicious sayings with customary designs for puppets. "Zither, chess, calligraphy and painted work," "orchid and peony" (representing promotion and wealth), and "pine, bamboo and plum blossom" (representing high morality) are all common designs on the garments and ornaments of scholar puppets; whereas on those of *laosheng* and *laodan* character puppets, there are always such designs as a bat and peaches (symbolizing possession of both happiness and longevity), and a *ruyi* (wishes coming true) and an elephant (auspicious).

Decorative designs on shadow-play sets, such as tables, desks, chairs, carriages and sedan-chairs, include "jade *ruyi* in a bottle" (symbolizing safety and good luck), "peony and sweet-scented osmanthus in a bottle" (signifying safety and wealth), "three halberds in a bottle" (wishing for promotion in rank), "five bats circling the Chinese character寿" (happiness and longevity), "a large cloud" (representing harmony), and so on. In Chinese tradition, decorative designs must have auspicious connotations. With their inventive minds, folk artisans constituted the audience's favored designs into shadow plays.

Table and chair: Qing Dynasty, Fengrun County, Hebei

Square tables for eight people: Qing Dynasty, Luanxian County, Hebei

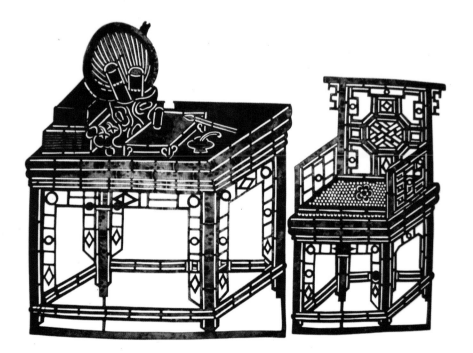

Table and chair: Qing Dynasty, collected by Tai Liping of Fengxiang County, Shaanxi

Imperial long table and chair: Qing Dynasty, Fengrun County, Hebei

Antique shelf: Qing Dynasty, Fengrun County, Hebei

Imperial chair and round table:
Qing Dynasty, Luanxian County, Hebei

Desk and stool: Qing Dynasty, collected by Tai Liping of
Fengxiang County, Shaanxi

Table and chair: Republic of China, collected by Zheng Quanming of
Linyi County, Shandong

Large seat for temporary rest: Qing Dynasty, Leting County, Hebei

Chairs with carved flower design:
Republic of China, Hebei

Long narrow table with carved flower design:
Republic of China, Hebei

Chair with carved flower design:
Republic of China, Hebei

Square table: Qing Dynasty,
Huaxian County, Shaanxi

Potted peach: Qing Dynasty,
Leting County, Hebei

Lotus vat: Qing Dynasty,
Luanxian County, Hebei

Carriage Designs

There are many carriage designs in the shadow play, like
the elephant-drawn carriage for the emperor's inspection
tours or carriages for his wife and concubines, carriages
for women of rich families, wagon for commoners, and
open wagon of peasants. These designs have moving
horse hooves and wheels. They are controlled by only two
operating sticks.

Elephant-drawn carriage for the emperor:
carved by Zhang Huazhou of Huaxian County, Shaanxi

Carriage: Qing Dynasty, Fengrun County, Hebei

Carriage: Qing Dynasty, Lulong County, Hebei

SHADOW PLAYS
IN THE 1960S AND 1970S

In the 1960s and 1970s, model Peking operas appeared in China. As they spread around the country after 1969, many shadow-play troupes began to perform these model operas with puppets, such as *Shajia Bang*, *Taking Tiger Mountain by Strategy*, and *The Story of the Red Lantern*.

The puppets were designed based on the popular characters in the Peking operas. Their ornamentation and costumes closely resembled those in real life. In many places, the puppet heads were made with transparent plastic, and the positive characters often had a pinkish hue on their faces to show their integrity. To accurately transplant the model operas into a shadow play, many troupes reformed lighting and sets. Methods such as painting distant views on plastic and setting secondary lights beyond the curtain were used.

Old couple:
Qinhuangdao Shadow Play Troupe

Woman Red Army soldier:
Changli Shadow Play Troupe,
Hebei

A Qing's wife in *Shajia Bang*:
Qinhuangdao Shadow Play Troupe

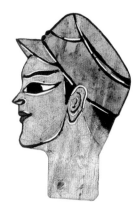

Soldiers of the Red Army (left) and the New Fourth Army:
Changli Shadow Play Troupe

Villagers: Qinhuangdao Shadow Play Troupe, Hebei

Foreigner: Qinhuangdao Shadow
Play Troupe

Eagle, a negative character in
Taking Tiger Mountain by Strategy:
Qinhuangdao Shadow Play Troupe

图书在版编目（CIP）数据

民间皮影：英文/魏力群编著．
—北京：外文出版社，2008
（中国民间文化遗产）
ISBN 978-7-119-04670-9
Ⅰ．民... Ⅱ．魏... Ⅲ．皮影—民间工艺—中国
—英文　Ⅳ.J528.3

中国版本图书馆 CIP 数据核字（2008）第 119616 号

出版策划：李振国
英文翻译：冯　鑫
英文审定：**Kris Sri Bhaggiyadatta**　韩清月
责任编辑：杨春燕
文案编辑：蔡莉莉　刘芳念
装帧设计：黎　红
印刷监制：韩少乙

本书由中国轻工业出版社授权出版

民间皮影

魏力群　编著

© 2008 外文出版社
出版发行：
外文出版社出版（中国北京百万庄大街 24 号）
邮政编码：100037
网　　址：www.flp.com.cn
电　　话：008610-68320579（总编室）
　　　　　008610-68995852（发行部）
　　　　　008610-68327750（版权部）
制　　版：
北京维诺传媒文化有限公司

印　　刷：
北京外文印刷厂

开　　本：787mm × 1092mm　1/16　印张：10.25
2008 年第 1 版第 1 次印刷
（英）
ISBN 978-7-119-04670-9
09800（平）
85-E-638 P